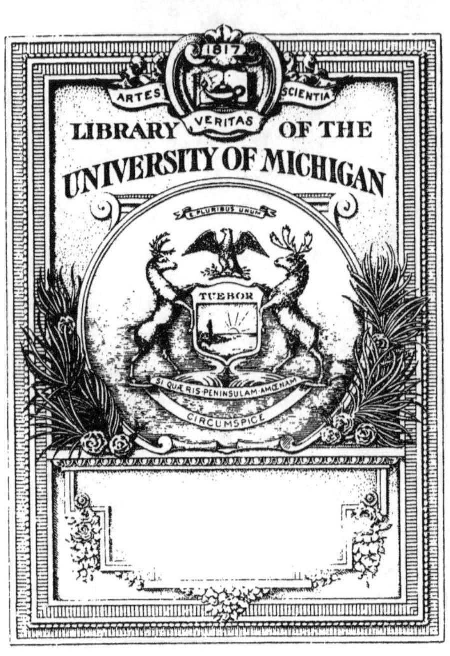
1817
ARTES
VERITAS
SCIENTIA
LIBRARY OF THE
UNIVERSITY OF MICHIGAN
E PLURIBUS UNUM
TUEBOR
SI QUÆRIS PENINSULAM AMŒNAM
CIRCUMSPICE

Agreement

between

Clothing Manufacturers of New York

and

Amalgamated
Clothing Workers of America

establishing an

Unemployment Insurance Fund

1928

FORM OF AGREEMENT

ESTABLISHING

UNEMPLOYMENT INSURANCE FUND

NEW YORK CLOTHING INDUSTRY

MEMORANDUM OF AGREEMENT, made this............................

day of .... by and between

....

(hereinafter called the Manufacturer) party of the first part, and the AMALGAMATED CLOTHING WORKERS OF AMERICA (hereinafter called the Union), party of the second part;

Witnesseth:

WHEREAS, arrangements are being entered into between the Manufacturer and the Union with reference to wages and working conditions; and similar arrangements are being entered into between the Union and other clothing Manufacturers in New York; and

WHEREAS, other agreements similar to this one are to be entered into between the Union and by all other clothing Manufacturers in New York City employing Union labor; and the parties hereto are desirous of mitigating the effect of unemployment;

NOW, THEREFORE, in consideration of the entering into the arrangements and agreements herein above recited and in consideration of the premises and of the mutual covenants herein contained, it is agreed by and between the parties hereto as follows:

ARTICLE I. The Manufacturer agrees to pay weekly, beginning with Sept. 1, 1928, to the Board of Trustees, one and one-half per cent of the total labor cost of all the clothing manufactured for him, whether his clothing is manufactured in his own inside shop or shops or in contract shops. By labor cost is meant the total weekly payroll of the Manufacturer's Union employees working in his inside shop plus total weekly payroll in contract shops applicable to his garments.

ARTICLE II. The obligation undertaken by the Manufacturer for the payment of sums to the Fund as provided for herein shall be on a parity with and as valid and enforceable as is his obligation to pay wages to his Union employees.

ARTICLE III. All sums so received shall be held in trust by the Board of Trustees subject to all the terms and conditions of this agreement, and such sums, and the income therefrom shall be held as a special Trust Fund, designated as "New York Clothing Unemployment Fund" hereinafter referred to as the "Fund." Payments from this Fund shall be made to members of the Union as unemployment benefits from time to time and under such terms and regulations as may be adopted hereafter by the Board of Trustees.

ARTICLE IV. No benefit which may accrue to any Union employee acquired by virtue hereof, can be assigned, transferred, alienated, hypothecated or bartered away, directly or indirectly, or be subject to attachment, garnishment, execution, sequestration, seizure, or other process. The Board of Trustees, or the Union, or any agency designated by it, may, however, pay any benefits to which a deceased Union employe might have been entitled to such person or persons as the Board shall in its absolute discretion determine, and no heir, next of kin, legal representative, creditor or claimant of any such decedent shall have any right or claim to any such benefits.

ARTICLE V. Neither the Manufacturer nor the Union shall have any right, property or interest in the Fund. Nor shall the Fund be subject to attachment, garnishment, execution, sequestration, seizure, or other process by reason of any claim on behalf of any person whatsoever against either the Manufacturer or the Union, or any Union employe.

ARTICLE VI. The Manufacturer and the Union agree at all times, during the continuance of this agreement, to keep such records as may be necessary for the proper administration of the Fund, and also to provide the Board of Trustees and the Union or its agency designated by it with such information and records as they may require or deem advisable for the proper performance of their duties.

ARTICLE VII. (a) This agreement shall be for the period of three years from June 30, 1928, to June 30, 1931.

(b) If (1) this agreement is not renewed at its expiration or if (2) the Manufacturer shall prior to the termination of this agreement cease to carry on business by dissolution, winding up, or in any way other than by sale, merger or consolidation, then upon the happening of either of these contingencies or the termination of this agreement, by lapse of time, or in any other way, the payments herein provided to be made to the Board of Trustees shall cease, but the Fund shall continue to be administered in the same manner in which it was administered during the life of this agreement, provided however that there is at least one agreement similar to the present still in force. In the event, however, that all agreements similar to the present and including the present are terminated in any way so that there is no remaining agreement in force, then the entire amount of the Fund shall be disposed of by distributing the Fund, as unemployment benefits, among Union employees in the industry in New York, within five years from the date of the termination of the last agreement.

ARTICLE VIII. If any law or ordinance is passed compelling the Manufacturer to contribute to any federal, state or municipal unemployment Fund with reference to any employees hereunder, the payments of the Manufacturer hereunder shall be reduced by the amount which the Manufacturer is compelled to pay to such federal, state, or municipal unemployment Fund. If the payment which the Manufacturer is compelled to make to any such Fund is equal to or greater than the payment required of the Manufacturer hereunder, then the obligation of the Manufacturer to make payment hereunder shall cease, and in such event the Fund shall be disposed of in the same manner herein provided for disposition at the expiration of this agreement.

ARTICLE IX. It is the intention and understanding of the parties to this agreement that there shall be one common Unemployment Fund for all the Manufacturers who may enter into similar Unemployment Fund agreements with the Union. This Fund shall have a single body of trustees which shall be selected as follows:

No more than three to be selected by the Union and no more than three to be selected by the New York Clothing Manufacturers' Exchange—(each shall appoint an equal number). The trustees selected by the Union for the Fund shall represent the Union under this agreement as well as under other Unemployment Fund agreements entered into with other clothing Manufacturers in New York; the trustees selected by the New York Clothing Manufacturers' Exchange shall represent the Manufacturer in this agreement, as well as in other Unemployment Fund agreements entered into with other clothing Manufacturers in New York. In addition to the trustees thus selected there shall be a Chairman of the Board of Trustees and the Impartial Chairman of the Clothing Industry in New York is hereby designated as Chairman of the Board of Trustees. He shall not be removable except by the joint act of the New York Clothing Manufacturers' Exchange and the Union. The number of trustees may be changed from time to time by the joint act of the New York Clothing Manufacturers' Exchange and the Union, but there shall not at any time be less than three (3) trustees nor more than seven (7), and the number of trustees shall at all times be odd.

ARTICLE X. (a) Any trustee may at any time resign from the trust hereby created by giving written notice of such resignation personally or by mail, addressed to the last known post office address of the remaining trustees. Should any of the trustees designated by the New York Clothing Manufacturers' Exchange die, resign, become incapacitated or unable or unwilling to act, or be removed, the vacancy so occurring shall be filled by the appointment of a successor to be named by the New York Clothing Manufacturers' Exchange. Should any of the trustees designated by the Union, die, resign, or become incapacitated or unwilling to act, or be removed, the vacancy so occurring shall be filled by the appointment of a successor to be named by the Union. All trustees appointed to fill any vacancy hereunder shall be vested with all the rights, powers and duties herein and hereby vested in their predecessors. Should the Chairman of the Board of Trustees, die, resign, be removed, become incapacitated, unable, unwilling or fail for any reason to act, then the vacancy so occurring shall be filled by the appointment of a successor named by the New York Clothing Manufacturers' Exchange and the Union, and if they are unable to agree upon such successor within a period of thirty (30) days, such vacancy shall be filled by the appointment of a person designated by Honorable Julian W. Mack. Until the appointment of a successor Chairman of the Board to fill such vacancy, the remaining trustees shall exercise all of the powers and perform all of the duties of the Board of Trustees. The appointment of any trustee hereunder shall be in writing delivered to the remaining trustees or their successors. If all the trustees designated by the Union or by the New

York Clothing Manufacturers' Exchange, as the case may be, shall not be present at any meeting of the trustees, the trustee or trustees designated by the New York Clothing Manufacturers' Exchange or the Union, as the case may be, present at such meeting, shall be entitled to cast as many votes or the same number of votes as the trustees designated by the other party present at said meeting shall be entitled to cast, it being the intention hereof that at any meeting of the trustees, regardless of the number present, the trustees representing the New York Clothing Manufacturers' Exchange and the trustees representing the Union shall have equal voting power.

(b) All questions that may arise or come before the trusteees shall be determined by the affirmative vote in person or by proxy or a majority of the trustees. Such vote may be given in meeting assembled or by a writing signed by the trustees, or by a majority of them, provided such writing is signed by one or more trustees designated by the Union, and one or more trustees designated by the New York Clothing Manufacturers' Exchange, and such decision or act of a majority of the trustees shall be binding and conclusive upon the parties hereto, the Board of Trustees and the Union employees. Any trustee may act by proxy. Any trustee may call a meeting of the Board of Trustees by giving at least five (5) days' notice in writing of the time of holding such meeting and having a copy thereof personally delivered to each trustee, or by mailing the same, postage prepaid, to the last known address of each trustee. Meetings of the Board of Trustees may be held at any time, without notice, if all of the trustees consent thereto.

(c) None of the trustees shall be entitled to compensation hereunder.

(d) Whenever the trustees or Board of Trustees are referred to herein, it is intended that such term shall include the trustees or Board of Trustees for the time being in office.

(e) The Board of Trustees shall keep true and accurate books of account and records which shall be audited by certified public accountants at least twice in each year.

(f) Each of the trustees shall be protected in acting upon any notice, request, consent, instruction, certificate, affidavit, resolution, opinion, receipt, application or other paper or document believed by him to be genuine and to have been made, executed or delivered by the proper party or by the proper authority, or authorities of the Union or Manufacturer, or by the party or parties purporting to have made, executed or delivered the same, and shall be protected in relaying and acting upon the opinion of legal counsel in connection with any matter pertaining to the carrying out of this agreement.

(g) Neither the trustees, nor any of their successors, shall be liable or responsible in respect to any action taken or omitted to be taken pursuant to any vote cast by the trustees, or any of them, or any proxy or proxies appointed hereunder, nor shall the trustees or any successor or successors, be liable for any loss occasioned by any act of commission or omission done or omitted to be done in good faith by them, or any of them, or of any proxy or proxies that may be appointed hereunder, nor for the acts of any agent, attorney or employee selected with reasonable care by them, or any of them, nor shall any trustee be liable for any act of omission or commission of any other trustee, or of any proxy or proxies, that may be appointed hereunder.

(h) The Board of Trustees shall have the power and authority to make reasonable rules and regulations, not inconsistent herewith, to carry out the provisions of this agreement, and shall have the right to make and adopt their own rules of procedure and action.

(i) The Board of Trustees shall be entitled to incur reasonable expenses for the purpose of carrying out the provisions of this agreement, which expenses shall be payable out of the Fund.

(j) Any question or dispute which may arise out of the interpretation or performance of the terms of this agreement or any part thereof between the parties hereto shall be determined by the Board of Trustees, acting for this purpose as arbitrators under the laws of New York; and such decisions shall be final and conclusive for all purposes whatsoever.

ARTICLE XI. This agreement and the terms and conditions of the trust hereby established may be modified at any time by the Board of Trustees, upon its obtaining the written consent of both the Union and the Manufacturer.

ARTICLE XII. (a) In the collection of payments to be made by the Manufacturer under the terms of this agreement for work done for him in contract shops, his payments shall be determined by the number of garments cut, by the price paid by the Manufacturer to the Contractor, and by the total weekly payroll of the contractor applicable to the garments of the Manufacturer.

(b) The Union or any agency designated by it shall receive the payments provided by this agreement to be made by the Manufacturer; the Union or its agency so designated by it shall collect the payroll sheets and such records as it may require of the Manufacturer as well as the weekly payroll records of the contractor; the Union or its agency so designated shall be in charge of paying the benefits under the provisions of this agreement from the Fund created thereby, all of which shall be subject to the supervision and control of the Board of Trustees.

(c) The expenses incurred by the Union or its agency so designated by it in carrying out the provisions of this agreement shall be payable out of the Fund.

ARTICLE XIII. This agreement may be extended or renewed by the joint written consent of the Manufacturer and the Union.

ARTICLE XIV. The trustees and the Chairman of the Board of Trustees, from time to time designated hereunder, shall evidence their acceptance of the trusts hereby created by executing this agreement or a duplicate thereof, and by such execution shall agree that they will in good faith and in all respects exercise the powers granted to them hereunder.

IN WITNESS WHEREOF the parties have caused this instrument to be duly executed the date first above written.

....
Manufacturer.

By ....

AMALGAMATED CLOTHING WORKERS
OF AMERICA

By ....

www.ingramcontent.com/pod-product-compliance
Lightning Source LLC
LaVergne TN
LVHW020638110826
845149LV00004B/1274

9781418190620